The Bones You Own

A Book About the Human Body

BY

BECKY BAINES

NATIONAL GEOGRAPHIC

Washington, D.C.

Right inside your body is the coolest puzzle of all!

patella

Your bones are shaped to fit together perfectly!

4

206 bones
that fit together and keep you standing tall.

NOW THAT'S TALL!

Your bones are the reason you can stand up straight.

They're in your chest and down your back...

Can you reach your back and feel the bumps of your spine?

vertebrae
(33 vertebrae bones connect to make your spine)

Many people can also feel their ribs. Can you count yours?

ribs

6

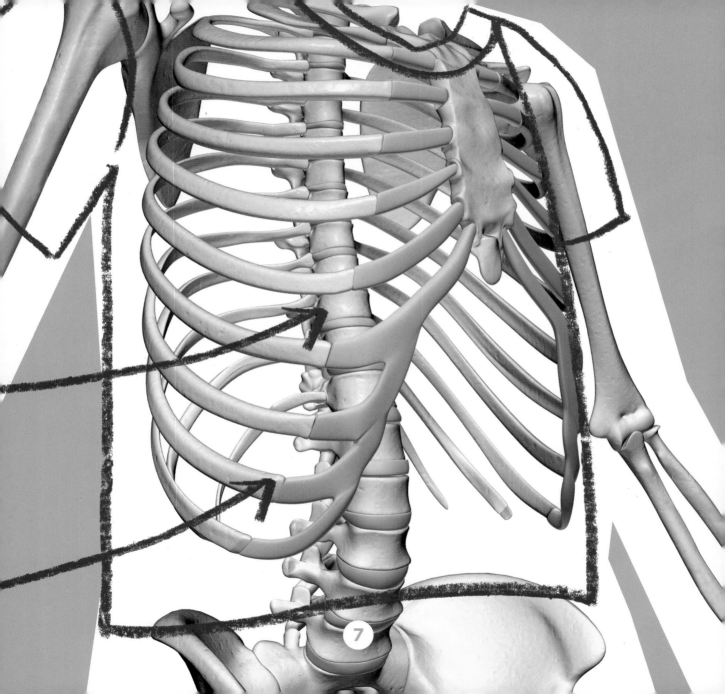

...your arms, and legs, and toes.

humerus

ulna

radius

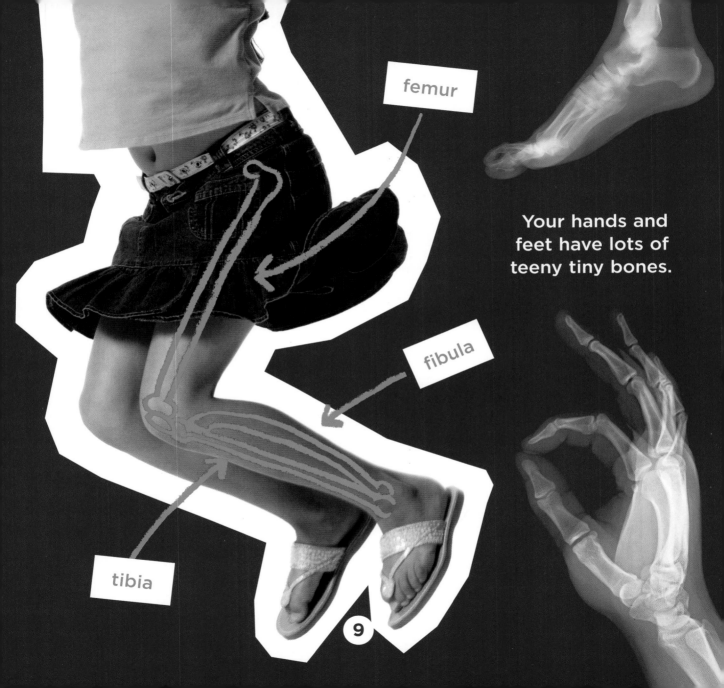

femur

fibula

tibia

Your hands and feet have lots of teeny tiny bones.

9

They're in your head, and ears,

mandible

incus, malleus, stapes

10

and mouth, and even half your nose!

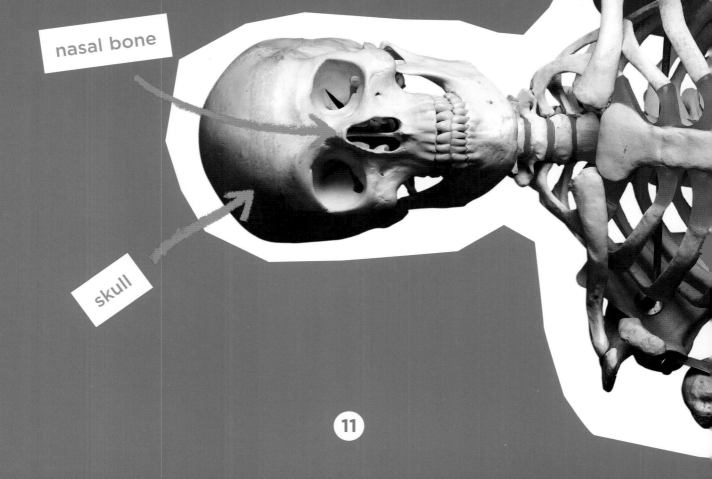

nasal bone

skull

Your bones protect soft body parts like brains, lungs, and squishy hearts...

Your ribs are like a chest guard to protect your heart.

12

...that fit
perfectly
inside you
like a living
work of art.

Your skull is
like a helmet
for your brain.

Your bones connect to let you move with joints in between.

The ends of some bones form joints. Some joints allow your bones to move around in a circle, like your shoulder.

Some joints allow straight moves, like your elbow.

14

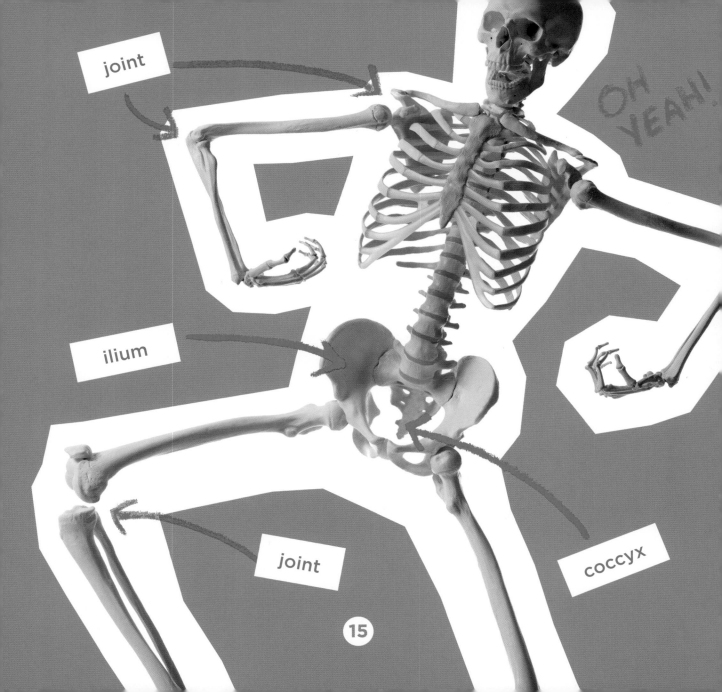

They can crack or break and then fix themselves, 'cause bones are living things!

X-rays can see through skin but not bone.

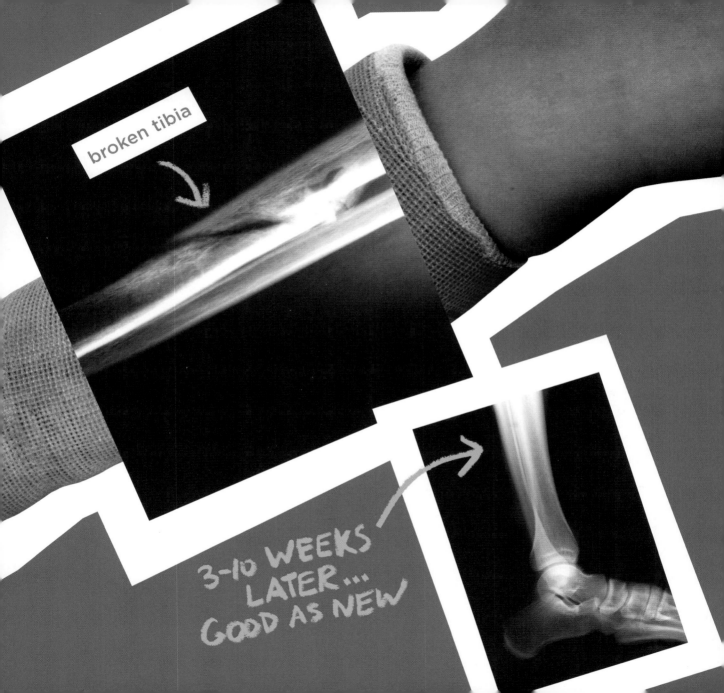

Your bones are white, smooth, and strong with jelly in the middle.

CAUTION: blood-making in progress

eewww!

bone marrow

Gushy, jelly-like part of the bone. It makes blood for the rest of your body!

compact bone

This is the hard part of bones. It's what you're looking at when you see a skeleton.

spongy bone

Spongy bone is lighter than compact bone.

19

Bones can be as long as your thigh

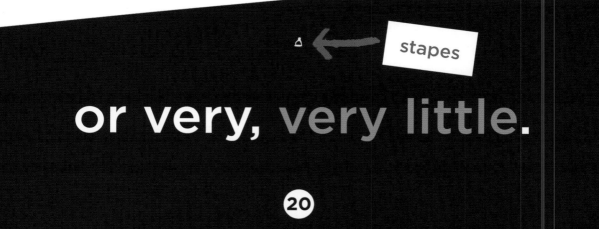

stapes

or very, very little.

femur

As you get older,
your bones get bigger.

LIFE-
SIZED!

When you
were born,
your bones
were soft.

When babies
are born, many
of their 300
bones are made
of cartilage.
(Your whole
outer ear
is cartilage
except your
lobe!)

They've hardened as you've grown.

CAREFUL.
IT'S SOFT!

When babies grow up, most cartilage is replaced with hard bone, which grows and glues itself together with other bones. That's why grown-ups only have 206 bones!

Sometimes bones are all that's left,

leaving clues
to life **unknown**.

Scientists know what
dinosaurs looked like
because of the bones
they've found.

25

Now look at this picture and try to remember

A Skeleton!

what's this?

what's this?

what's this?

the names of the bones you own!

27

Zigzag through these ideas for more thoughts about your bones.

Do you know where your funny bone is?

What would you look like without bones?

Try walking without bending ANY joints!

You have 400 joints that help you bend. Can you bend them all?

X-RAY

Have you ever seen an x-ray of your bones?

The stapes is the littlest bone in your body. Where is it? Hint: the answer's in this book.

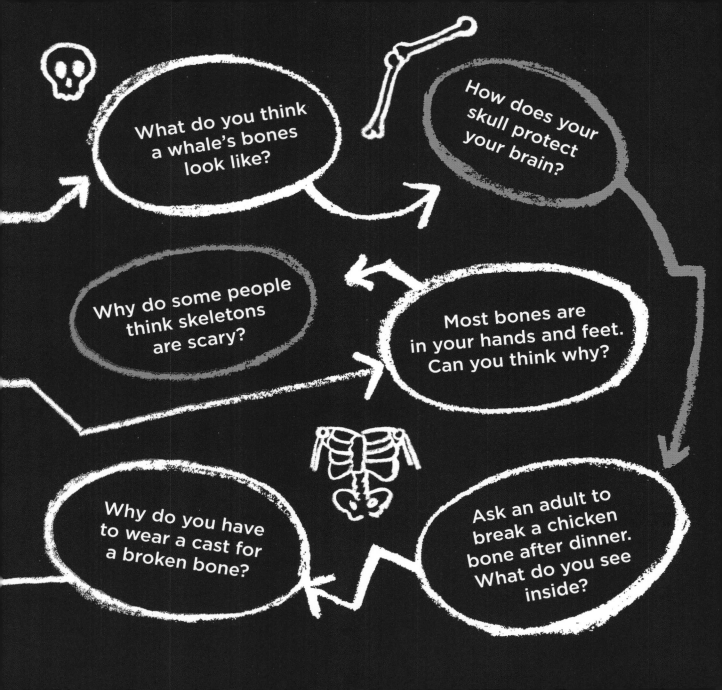

National Geographic's net proceeds support vital exploration, conservation, research, and education programs.

Published by the National Geographic Society
1145 17th Street, N.W.
Washington, D.C. 20036
Visit us online at www.nationalgeographic.com/books

Design: fuszion

Printed in the United States of America

Library of Congress Cataloging-in-Publication Data

Baines, Rebecca.
   The Bones You Own :
A Book About the Human Body /
by Becky Baines.
     p. cm. — (Zig zag)
     ISBN 978-1-4263-0410-1 (hardcover : alk. paper) —
ISBN 978-1-4263-0411-8 (lib. bdg. : alk. paper)
1. Bones. 2. Skeleton. I. Title.
QM101.B346 2009
612.7'5--dc22
2008047900

Photo Credits
Corbis: 7
Getty: 4, 5, 8, 9, 10, 12, 14, 16, 18, 19, 23, 27
iStock: 4, 6, 9, 11, 17
Jupiterimages: 24
Masterfile: 6, 15, 20

To my grandparents,
who love every bone
in my body.
—B.B.